Personal Finance Your Way

S. M. Green

DEDICATION

This book is dedicated to those who have a desire to take control of your personal finance. Although there are many agencies and resources that offer assistance in managing your credit card payments as well as assistance during times of crisis, my goal is to empower you to assess, manage, and control your finance, not from a template but, based on your household income and resources – your way.

CONTENTS

Legal disclaimer and acknowledgements

This book is provided as an informational resource only and to provide an overview of personal finances. All references included are provided as the most current information available at the time of this writing. Understanding how things are ever changing, please be aware that some content may have changed or been deleted since originally published.

I do not receive any compensation from any of the services or resources mentioned in this book but instead am committed to sharing interesting and entertaining information that I have personally taken advantage of or have received positive feedback from others.

The author/publisher specifically disclaim liability, loss, or risk that is incurred as an outcome, directly or indirectly, through the use and application of any contents of the work.

End User Rights

Start from the Beginning – Assess Your Financial Health

When you or a family member are feeling ill, you don't hesitate to make an appointment to the doctor's office. Once you arrive, they ask you various questions, sometimes draw blood, or may even need to order x-rays or tests, depending on your illness, before they can begin treating you. In the same manner, from time to time we need to assess our financial health to gauge if a "treatment plan" is needed to get it back into prime condition.

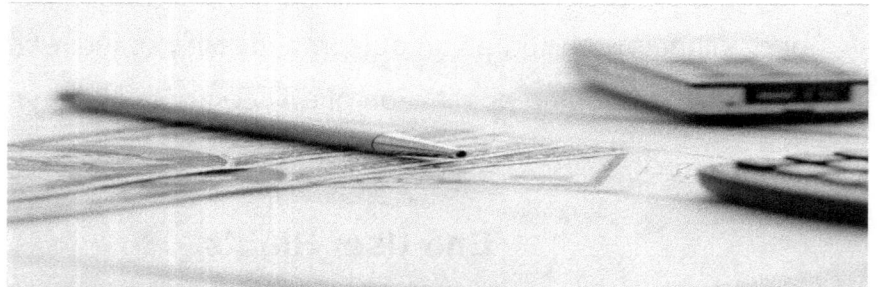

Faced with the challenges of an unsteady economy, high unemployment, increasing layoffs, a rise in student loan debt, credit card debt, and an unstable stock market, more and more consumers must re-evaluate their personal finances and make changes to avoid default, repossessions, foreclosures, and/or bankruptcy. Just as many of us are diligent in managing our physical health through annual doctor visits, we should also assess our financial health on a continuous basis to adjust for unexpected and unplanned life changes.

The following are four simple steps to help you obtain an overall picture of your monthly income and expenses. Once done, you will be better prepared to move forward in planning and executing an effective personal financial plan.

Step One: Gather ALL of Your Bills. Pull together copies of everything that you owe from mortgage payments to outstanding doctor's bills. With more and more companies going "paperless", remember to print off any online statements that you receive, including your most recent bank statement.   Separate these bills, both paper and electronic, into two stacks - one for "monthly household expenses" and one for "credit cards, installments, and loans". Use the bank statement to document you monthly expenses for food and other incidentals. Don't forget to account for monthly fees, regardless of how small, that you are charged such as bank fees. Incredibly these fees can add up and throw off your budget completely.

Step Two: Document Household Expenses and Debts. Having a clear picture of your monthly income and expenses allows you to be better suited to identify areas where reductions may be necessary as well as seeing, at a glance, if your monthly income is sufficient to maintain current expenses. Microsoft Office has a variety of templates available to track expenditures that can be downloaded or printed. If you are familiar with Excel, download the Excel template as it contains formulas already implanted that will calculate as you enter the information. Save the Excel document on your computer or laptop and enter income and expenses under the appropriate category. Resources of this sort are available online for free from basic to elaborate worksheets. I encourage you to find the best one to captures your types of expenses and save it for future use. .

Step Three: Document Expenses that are paid Semi-Annually or Annually. There are several expenses that are only paid annually or semi-annually such as auto registration, inspections, property taxes, and even some insurance. These expenses are considered variable fixed expenses. To determine the monthly expense of these items, multiple the total by 12 (annually) or 6 (semi-annually) and enter the total for that expense. (Example: Auto registration is $102 annually – 102 divided by 12 is $8.50 (monthly expense). Again, remember that even though the expense may seem small, if not included you will not obtain a truly accurate representation of your financial picture.

Step Four: Document All Monthly Income Received.

After entering all of your expenses, you will now look at your monthly income and resources. Document your total take-home pay from all sources including wages, alimony, child support, and any others. If you receive rent from others, include it. If you have a home based business, enter the average monthly income you receive, if any. Even if you receive a monthly allowance or stipend from someone else, it should be included.

EXCEPTION: Any monthly income currently being received that is expected to end within the next six months does not have to be included unless you plan to revise your budget once that income source has ended.

You're Done!

After completing these simple steps you should be able to determine, at a glance, if you are bringing in enough money to cover your expenses, where your money is going and where changes can be made to help you get into a better financial position.

Know Your Debt to Income Ratio

<u>Imagine the following scenario</u>:

Sara Jones is a single, employed woman with a gross (before taxes) monthly income of $4,000. She pays her rent of $1,000 on time every month. Sara has several credit cards with payments totaling $350, but they are not delinquent because she makes sure to send in the payment due each month, even if some payments are a little late. She also has a student loan payment of $100 each month. Sara's car payment each month is $400. Sara decides that she would like to begin looking for a home and applies for a loan through her bank but is turned down for the loan. She wonders, "How can I be turned down when I pay my bills each month?"

In all likelihood, after pulling Sara's credit report and looking at the debt-to-income ratio, the bank surmised that Sara posed a high credit risk and would be less likely to repay the loan. Many financial institutions agree that your debt to income ratio should not exceed 36% of your gross monthly income. In the scenario above, the total monthly debt is $1850. To establish your debt-to-income ratio, divide your monthly debt payment by your monthly income. The end result is your debt-to-income ratio.

Monthly income: $4,000

Monthly debt payment: $1,850

Debt-to-income ratio: $1,850/$4,000 = 46%

If you have a ratio of 30% or less, it means you have a great debt-to-income ratio, which means that your income is significantly more than what you owe. However, if you have a debt-to-income ratio of 44% or higher, it means you are taking on too much debt in relation to your income, in the eyes of mortgage lenders and other creditors. Even though there may be some lenders willing to offer a home loan to high risk consumers, the interest rate is usually very high.

A simple formula to calculate your debt-to-income ratio (DTI) is to take your monthly long-term recurring debt payments such as your rent/mortgage, credit cards, auto, insurance premiums, student loans, alimony, child support, and government liens and divide the total by your monthly income. Any debt that will be paid off within six months by making your normal payment does not need to be included in your total debt payments. Monthly food expenses, utilities, and other expenses are not included in the debt-to-income ratio. Even though you will definitely want to budget for these expenses, they are not used by lenders when calculating your DTI.

Wondering what to do if your debt-to-income ratio is too high? Two options are available, increase income or reduce expenses. In the next section we will begin developing a workable budget and find creative ways to free up money and reduce your overall debt.

Lenders calculate your debt-to-income ratio to determine how much mortgage you can afford. Even if you are a current homeowner and consider refinancing for a lower interest rate, DTI is looked at when determining if you qualify. What better feeling is there than to go in knowing that your debt-to-income ratio is strong? Of course, this is only one step in strengthening your financial health. We will look at how credit and credit scores play a big part in obtaining loans later.

Identify and Address Priorities - Needs

When reviewing monthly household expenses, it is important to identify those areas that are considered priorities such as mortgage or rent, food, utilities, transportation, and insurance. One of the most challenging areas is separating the "needs" from the "wants". We "need" shelter, food, clothing, electricity, gas, water, a way to get to and from work, insurance (health, auto, etc.) and an emergency savings. We "want" cable television, internet service, smartphones and other electronics, to go out to eat, and to go to movies and other entertainment. In this article we will look at ways to manage our "needs" so that we can free up money to afford some of the "wants" in our lives.

Housing: Even though housing costs are fixed monthly expenses, there are ways that you can still manage them to be better aligned with your finances. According to the Federal Reserve your monthly housing costs, including rent or mortgage, taxes, interest and insurance should not exceed 28% of your monthly pre-tax income. For example a person making $50,000 annually, which equates to approximately $4,167 pre-tax income per month, the total housing cost should not exceed more than $1,167 to be considered safe. (4,167 x 0.28 = 1,167) Homeowners that have housing costs that are too high, can contact the mortgage company to see if refinancing for a lower interest rate can help in reducing the monthly mortgage costs. Renters may want to check with the rental agency to see if a more cost effective option is available once their lease agreement ends.

Food: According to an article published by NaturalNews.com, US food prices increased by 19% in 2014 due to drought and rising inflation. The USDA recommends $150-$175 monthly per person in a household to be allocated in determining food costs. For many people who have experienced layoffs or reductions in pay, this monthly cost can seem high. To better manage your food costs, consider devoting time to plan meals by the week, making your shopping list from your meal plan. You can often buy in bulk and separate meats to cover several meals. Go online and search for coupons that can be printed and redeemed at your local store. My children and I often challenge ourselves to come up with meals for a family of four for $10 or less. (One excellent example is Shrimp Alfredo – 1 lb. shrimp ($3.99 on sale), Alfredo sauce ($1.50), Fettuccini noodles (1.50), 1 bag of Salad mix ($1.00) and garlic toast ($2.00) ---- Total $9.99)

Utilities: If you haven't done so recently, contact each of your utility providers in your area for special deals that may save you hundreds of dollars each month. Ask you current electric provider if they offer average billing, which looks at your costs over the previous twelve months and allocates an average amount monthly that can greatly reduce your costs during off seasons. If any of your utility bills seem unusually high, contact the provider and ask what you can do to reduce your monthly costs. Unplugging chargers and small appliances when not in use and setting the air or heat to come on 30 minutes before you arrive home from work can make a big difference in electricity costs.

Transportation: Over the past several years the cost of gasoline has greatly increased putting more and more strain on monthly finances. In large metropolitan areas many companies offer "ride shares" among employees with similar work schedules. Some companies provide bus or train passes at reduced costs to employees that wish to "park and ride". If you company offers flexible work schedules, consider telecommuting several days per week to cut costs. Consider trading in an existing vehicle for one that offers better gas mileage and lower monthly costs. Commute to and from work with a spouse that works similar hours to avoid driving two cars. Think creatively on other ways to manage your transportation costs – the possibilities are almost endless.

Insurance: Many companies offer group health insurance for employees and their families but with the new healthcare laws, remain open to researching other affordable options that may be available to you. In the event of a layoff or termination, costs associated with maintaining your group health insurance through COBRA may double and event triple since the "employer paid" portion would become your responsibility.

If you are a renter, consider renter's insurance. It is not very expensive and can be added onto one of your existing insurance policies. With accidental fires, burglaries, and other unforeseen instances, it is highly recommended that you obtain renter's insurance to cover your belongings to help you start over, if needed.

Auto insurance, if you own a car, is another area where you should periodically "shop" around for better deals that often can offer more benefits than you currently have at a cheaper rate. Most states require that you have full coverage insurance on your auto if you are still paying a lender for the car. Liability only coverage will take care of the other vehicle if you are in an accident but not yours.

Funeral costs are something many of us would rather not think about but it should be identified when developing an effective financial plan. Check the average costs in your area for services and burials and consider getting the minimum policy to save your family from worrying during a difficult time. Remember you can always increase the coverage amount when you can afford it to allow for extra funds to go towards final expenses and outstanding bills.

Savings: Based on everything that has been done so far, it is likely that you should see a reduction in your monthly household expenses and be able to begin an emergency savings. I always recommend that a person start with a very small amount, maybe $25 to $50, each pay period and set up direct deposit into a savings account. Most banks will allow you to have more than one savings account so I recommend a separate emergency account that does not have a bank card associated with it. Your goal is to not have to withdraw any money from this account unless it is for a true emergency.

During a seminar I attended a year ago at the Federal Reserve Bank, one of the speakers emphasized the importance of establishing a savings and suggested an online source, which I tried, called SmartyPig. The account can be opened with as little as $25 and give options to set several goals such as vacation, graduation, and emergency and determine a date when you would like to meet that goal. The system calculates the monthly amount that will be needed to be deposited to reach your goal within the allocated timeline and gives an option for automatic deposits from a bank account or manual deposits that you make with a debit card. When you need the money, you have several options of withdrawing as well. I loved it because once I made my initial deposit; I didn't have to worry about making sure I stayed on schedule. I reached my preset goal and was very happy with the overall experience. When thinking about saving options, look online for some of the newer products being offered by many of the major banking institutions, some even allow you to earn interest on your money while you save.

As you can see, I tried to touch on some of the "needs" that all of us have. Others may have areas that are considered a "need" versus a "want" that is not mentioned, but use the same philosophy as with these. Think outside the box; ask yourself "can I reduce this cost in any way".

Identify and Address Priorities – Recurring Debt

As we continue to develop our customized budget, the focus now will be on credit card debt and installment loans. In this section we will look closely at each type of debt and determine options on reducing and/or paying off the debt in a timelier manner, freeing up more discretionary funds for savings or other debts. Identify those debts that are not considered monthly household expenses such as credit card bills, collection notices, medical bills, and student loans. For each one, write down the creditor (who you owe), the account number, due date, minimum payment (if any), and contact phone number for their billing or customer service department. Follow the steps below for each type of creditor that you have.

Credit Card Bills: Many people often pay only the minimum due shown on credit card statements because it works within their individual budgets. A small balance of $200 could take several years to pay off by paying only the minimum because of the interest and late fees charged. Contact the credit card company and ask about any hardship program they may offer that can sometimes reduce the interest rate for several months so that more of your payments can be applied to the principal. Also ask about changing the due date to coincide better with your pay schedule, which reduces the chance of being charged late fees. If no help is offered, take control of the debt to pay it off as quickly as possible. Interest is charged generally on the balance, so check to see what your interest rate is (shown on your statement) and make sure the payment amount covers the interest and extra towards bringing the balance down. Be sure to check if more than one interest rate is being charged since some credit card companies charge one interest rate for charges and another rate for cash advances.

Collection Accounts: Unlike credit cards, accounts that have gone to collection do not charge interest or late fees so the balance does not go up. Many collection companies will offer affordable repayment plans, which may fit in your budget. Some will offer a one-time settlement (usually half of what is owed) and forgive the remainder of the balance. Before accepting a settlement offer, always ask how a repayment plan and/or settlement will be reported to the credit bureau. Even though the debt may already show delinquent on your credit report, upon payment you would want them to report it as "paid in full". Ask for a written statement on the terms that you have agreed upon.

Also keep in mind that many collection agencies

purchase your debt from creditors, which is frowned upon by the Federal Trade Commission. After several months, many creditors charge-off the debt and may send it to their in-house collection department. This is more preferable than dealing with a third party collection agency. If you receive harassing calls from a collector, consider contacting the FTC to see what recourse may be available to you.

Medical Bills (not already gone to collection): Many physicians, hospitals, and labs have in-house billing departments. By simply contact these billing departments, small payments or even deferred payments can be arranged to pay these off in a relatively short amount of time. Also don't be afraid to ask if you have a credit on your account that can be applied to an outstanding balance. Many times I have discovered sizable credits on dental and medical accounts after insurance claim payments have been processed.

Student Loans and IRS Debt: Contacting the servicer of student loans can often result in a deferred payment plan or reduction of loan payments until your financial situation improves. In the same way, contacting the IRS for assistance in paying owed taxes will not only give you affordable payments but also prevent wage garnishment which requires larger payments to be taken directly out of your paycheck and be paid in full within a shorter period of time. If you happen to owe a large amount to the IRS, go to IRS.gov and consider the Offer in Compromise, which if accepted, could greatly reduce your IRS debt.

Update your *Monthly Household Expense Worksheet* to reflect the new payments that you have successfully negotiated and celebrate another step completed toward your financial well-being. Remember that no matter how overwhelming these debts may seem avoidance is your worst enemy. My grandmother often reminded me that "a closed mouth will never get fed". I've passed this on for many years, don't be afraid to open your mouth and ask for help.

We will review "wants" in the next section. You'll be happy to know you can still have most of the things you want with just a little planning.

Identify and Address Priorities - Wants

As mentioned in the previous section, "wants" can include non-essential services or items such as cable television, internet service, smartphones and other electronics, going out to eat, and going to movies and other entertainment. If you have identified your current monthly expenses, monthly income, and looked at ways to reduce the monthly costs of essential "needs", you should have a better idea of how much discretionary income is remaining that can be applied to some or all of the non-essential things that you desire. We will apply the same process to items that fall under the category of "wants" just like we looked for creative ways to reduce the cost spent on monthly "needs".

Cable Television:

All of us would like to have the option to have additional television channels that are tailored to our interests. Some of those channels could include the Food Network, Sports Channel, CNN, and even movie channels like Showtime, HBO, and Cinemax. The cost of these additional channels can greatly increase your basic cable television package.

Many of the providers offer attractive promotions that can lure you into what seems like a great deal, but could turn into a nightmare if you aren't careful in understanding the terms of the promotion. If you are offered free channels for the first three months of signing up, be sure to contact the provider and cancel those premium channels that would result in a sizeable bill going forward. Consider choosing only one of the movie channels and ask for individual price quotes for the additional premium channels (after the promotion period) and choose according to your financial ability.

Internet Service:

Being able to access the Internet has become more and more needed for research for children's school work as well as many careers that offer flexible work schedules. Be diligent in searching for an Internet provider and keep in mind that you do not have to "bundle" with another service to get a good deal. Recently when reviewing my own cable and internet providers (which was the same provider at one time); I realized a $50 savings per month by separating the services between two providers. (The money saved was re-directed to another area of my finances such as savings or a bill).

Smartphones:

In today's times we all need to be able to stay in touch with family, friends, and our jobs when on the go. The cost of smartphones can be very expensive if you're trying to get the top-of-the-line but when you consider how often a "new, better version" comes out, why waste all that money? In choosing you cell phone and carrier, shop around. Consider all of the options available and ask yourself if you really need to be able to go on the Internet from your phone or other things that can be accomplished on your computer, laptop, or tablet. Yes, the new gadgets are great but think about the money you can save. If you must have a smartphone, maybe for work or some other reason, rather than purchase a new one, shop online at the larger providers for one that has been refurbished or marked down on clearance to make room for the newer models. The market has become very competitive and smart phones are available for as little as $50 per month through some providers.

Other Electronics:

I'll admit that my family is definitely an "electronics" family with five sons, but even in that area I have become very creative in purchasing those items that they really want. The game consoles are the big thing in my home and we all know how pricey they can be. Take advantage of shopper rewards such as "Game Stop's PowerUp Rewards". For a $14 annual membership fee, I receive discounts on games and consoles and points that can be used towards $10, $20, $30 off. When new games are expected to be released, consider putting a $5 deposit down to hold the game, which ensures you will receive it on the first day of release. Usually you will have several months before the game is released, so we just pay on it every two weeks and most times the games are paid in full by the time the release date rolls around. Other electronics such as tablets and MP3 players are easy to find online for a fraction of the cost that you will pay in a store. One website that I utilized over Christmas that saved me a lot of money was "NoMoreRacks.com" where I was able to find Leap Pads for my grandchildren, tablets for less than $100 for my nieces, and other great finds. Visit your favorite retailer's online website where a great deal on "web only" prices can be found.

Movies:

One of my older sons stopped by one day and mentioned that he and his girlfriend had gone to see the latest movie that had just come out. Out of curiosity I asked how much it costs. I was amazed at how expensive the tickets are now and adding in food items, the bill was more than I was willing to pay. You see, I can't remember the last time I have gone to the movies and paid full price. Why would I when there are so many options available. Groupon.com offers movie deals to various theatres almost weekly. (You just select your location and they show what deals are available – groupon.com/Dallas, groupon.com/Atlanta, etc.) We usually will purchase the $5 (movie and drink) package and get enough to go several times. Another option has been to look on the individual theatre websites for special promotions for upcoming holidays and events. We have also started having movie night at home that has turned into a monthly tradition where we will get a movie from Redbox ($3) or order a $6 movie from our cable television provider (which is a lot less than purchase multiple movie tickets at full price), make snacks and enjoy the movie.

Going Out to Eat or Other Entertainment:

I mentioned Groupon.com in the movie section above, but you will be amazed at the other great deals we find under the various categories. There are sections for dining, entertainment, and even trips. Also check with your local Visitors Bureau who may offer passes and booklets, for a fee, that covers a lot of the local attractions admission fees and other services. Going out doesn't have to be expensive, you just need to begin thinking creatively about where you're going and check online to see if there are any promotions going on.

Remember: Every penny saved counts!

After completing some or all of the above suggested remedies, you will find that you feel better informed and equipped to continue managing your finances effectively for you and your family. Even though there will be some expenses that cannot be reduced by much, by reducing those that you can make a big difference on your overall financial health.

Begin the Process of Becoming Debt Free

Earlier I touched on credit card debt and installment loans that may take 10 – 20 years to pay in full with minimum and late payments. Having debt is not a bad thing but it must be managed properly or it can get out of hand fast. Early in my life I decided to not incur any long-term debt and saved money until I could pay for things in full. As I got older, I realized that by not having any credit, lenders looking to give me a loan for a car or anything large did not have a payment history to determine their risk. This resulted in being charged a higher interest rate and subsequently paying more for the purchase than someone with a better credit score.

Even if you feel you are currently managing your monthly credit card and loan payments, many consumers are seeing the benefits of becoming debt-free and having only one or two emergency credit cards. As a former employee of a major credit counseling agency, I would recommend one option to consider when moving towards becoming debt-free. By contacting the National Foundation for Credit Counseling (NFCC) you will have access to a nation-wide list of member agencies that offer free or low cost budget counseling, which includes a review of your monthly income, expenses and current debts and offers a proposed plan of paying off the recurring debt in less than 5 years. For consumer convenience these services can be offered over the phone as well as face-to-face in your local geographic area. These agencies, most often, have negotiated agreements with credit card companies and other creditors to stop the interest and accept a proposed monthly amount based on your current balance. As mentioned, the counseling session is generally free or low cost but if you decide to pay off your debts through one of these agencies, you may be charged a small monthly administrative fee and one set amount to pay each month until each debt is paid in full. (**PLEASE NOTE**: Many creditors will report these debts as "paid through a third party" on your credit report if you go through an agency).

If you are disciplined and can commit to following the steps below to be debt free, you can accomplish this yourself without going to a credit counseling agency. These steps will help you become debt-free within 3-5 years, depending on your budget and credit balance.

1. If you have not done so already, write down the names, account number, phone number, and balance for each

credit card and loan payment that you have. Beside each account write the interest rate that is being charged, if any. If you have an auto loan or any other secured loan, the payment amounts cannot be reduced but can be added to your list to pay off early.

2. At this point, call each creditor and request a reduced interest rate. Explain that you are budgeting and would like to begin paying down your debt. If they are willing to reduce the interest, write down the new interest rate for each. If asked, you DO NOT want to close these accounts. Simply chose one credit card (or two) to keep for emergencies and travel, and then lock the others away. When looking at your credit report, many creditors will look to see what your available credit line is, which helps your overall score.

3. Looking at your balance for each account, divide your annual percentage rate by 12 to get the monthly percentage rate. (Example: Annual percentage rate is 15% - 0.15/12 = **0.0125**). Multiply the balance by your monthly percentage rate. The result will be how much interest you would pay on that balance for one month. (Example: Balance is $2,500 x 0.0125 = **$31.25**)

4. In the step above, after calculating the interest rate for an account with a $2,500 balance you see that $31.25 of your payment would go towards interest. If you have reduced other household expenses and have more than the minimum payment available, the payment should be double the interest ($60.00) to account for the interest and balance. In this example, the total amount of interest charged on a balance of $2,500 with a 15% interest rate is approximately $375 for one year if you do not make any more charges on that card. By paying the proposed payment of $60.00 per month for this account it would take approximately 47-48 months (4 years) to pay off this debt.

5. Follow Step 3 for each credit card or loan account with an interest rate. For those accounts that do not have an interest rate (collection account, medical bills, etc.) simply divide the balance by 12 to have them paid in full within one year, or if the balance is large, divide by 24 to pay off within two years.

6. At this point, total your new monthly payment amounts. This will be the amount that you will set aside to pay off

your debts each month. I would suggest implementing the "snowball effect" in becoming debt free faster. Often referred as the "snowball effect", once an account is paid off, the payment that was going to that account should be divided up among the other accounts evenly, if possible. Do this for each account as it is paid in full, which will result in the accounts with the largest balance being able to pay off quite a bit faster.

7. At any time during the process, you can increase the payments being sent to a particular creditor to pay that debt off faster and move on to the next one. Remember you're in control.

By following these steps, you will be amazed at how quickly you will begin to see the balances go down. It is also very important to look at each monthly statement to be sure your payment was processed correctly and update you balances. If you have any questions or see additional fees being charged, contact the creditor and request a change of due date to avoid late fees and ask if any late fees can be waived.

Whenever you received extra money (a gift, bonus, or tax refund), consider putting it towards your debt payments to pay off even faster. Once done, the money that you have been paying for credit card and loan debt each month can be put into a savings account for added financial security.

Saving – Thinking Outside the Box

With everything that's going on in our busy lives, it's often difficult to think about saving money for emergencies, college, or vacations. Many people believe that they do not make enough money to save. One thing that is definite, there will be something that happens, out of nowhere, that will require money that is not within your budget. It could be costly auto repairs or a sudden illness that requires a hospital stay or even a malfunctioned appliance that has to be replaced immediately. Since we cannot plan for these unexpected occurrences, it is a wise financial move to set money aside monthly to be better positioned to handle whatever may come up.

There is no set amount that you should have saved away for emergencies, but most experts suggest at least a 6-month reserve of total monthly expenses. For instance, if your monthly expenses are $3,625, you would need to have at least $21,750 set aside in a savings account. The premise is that if you are hurt, disabled, or laid off from work, it may take you at least six months to get back to work fulltime and during that time, your monthly bills will continue to be paid on time. Quite naturally, not many of us have $21,750 available to put aside until we need it, but by beginning to put aside small investments each month towards a savings account you can set your own goal for each savings account you open.

After you have developed your budget and determine how much discretionary funds are available after paying your monthly expenses, start by making a commitment to allocate at least 10% of what is left over towards an emergency savings. This is a safe figure to start with and can always be increased if you're able to. The key to a successful savings is to put away funds that you will not access for any reason other than what it is allocated for. In my experience, it has been best to open a separate savings account across town that is not readily accessible, which would deter me from withdrawing money unless absolutely necessary. That savings account should not have a debit card associated with it and if it does come with one, lock it away and do not carry it on your person. (Unless you're really disciplined, the temptation is too great knowing you have money available). Another option is to open an online savings account, preferably one that pays interest. Many of the financial institutions such as Chase, Bank of America, Comerica, and others offer these products with a minimal amount required to open, usually less than $100.

Check with local credit unions who often offer products that allow you to deposit a set amount, through direct deposit, on a monthly basis towards a specific goal. As you reach the goal. you are given the option to receive the total amount or continue saving. This method is especially helpful for setting a small amount aside all year for Christmas gifts or annual events.

For those who may have a very limited amount of discretionary funds available after paying your monthly expenses, look closely at things that you are spending on to find additional money for saving. Some examples include:

1. Smokers often purchase one pack of cigarettes per cay (or) one pack every other day. Total the cost for the month and consider reducing that cost by half and save the rest.

2. Coffee drinkers often have their routine stops in the morning. Calculate how much it costs for your cup of coffee and add it up for the month. Consider making coffee at home and "splurge" once or twice a month on the gourmet coffee.

3. Those of you who go out to eat for lunch each day spend, on an average $7-$10 per day. Consider making lunches and save most of the money spent on fast foods.

4. If you live close to a co-worker or your spouse works similar hours as you, consider driving one week and

the other driving the next week. Use the money that you would have used for gas and place it in a savings.

5. Plan meals ahead of time so that you can purchase meats and vegetables in bulk. Separate and label meats for planned meals. We have been able to save quite a bit on groceries by adhering to this plan.

These are just a few examples of how you can "find" some extra money to begin your savings. Once your savings account begins to grow, you'll become more and more motivated to keep it up.

Fair Housing – Know Your Rights

Imagine this: *You're looking for an apartment to rent and was told by the leasing agent they do not accept people with children. Or you are considering purchasing a home in a suburban area and the real estate agent discourages you from selecting a home in a certain area because you may not fit in with the neighbors. What if you have a disability and require assistance from a guide dog but are told that the apartment is not handicap accessible and does not allow animals?* All of these instances and more have occurred in the past, which prompted a law to be enacted to protect the rights of consumers with regard to housing.

Most are not aware that the federal Fair Housing Act prohibits discrimination in the sale, rental, and financing of dwellings and in other housing-related transactions, based on race, color, national origin, religion, sex, disability, and family status. The U. S. Department of Housing and Urban Development (HUD) has the responsibility to administer and enforce the provisions of the Fair Housing Act. The Act covers most housing but in some circumstances exempts owner-occupied buildings with no more than four units, single-family housing sold or rented without the use of a broker, and housing operated by an organization or private club that limit occupancy to members only.

If you are interested in purchasing a home or renting home/apartment: It is prohibited, by law, for anyone to refuse to rent or sell housing; refuse to negotiate for housing; make housing available; deny a dwelling; set different terms, conditions or privileges for sale or rental of a dwelling; provide different housing services or facilities; falsely deny that housing is available for inspection, sale, or rental; persuade owners to sell or rent; or deny anyone access to a membership in a facility or service related to the sale or rental of housing based on race, color, national origin, religion, sex, family status, or disability.

When dealing with mortgage lenders: It is prohibited, by law, for a lender to refuse to make a mortgage loan, refuse to provide information regarding loans, impose different terms or conditions on a loan such as different interest rates, points or fees, discriminate in appraising property, refuse to purchase a loan, or set different terms or conditions for purchasing a loan based on race, color, national origin, religion, sex, family status, or disability.

If you or someone associated with you has a disability: A disability is defined, in these circumstances as, having a physical or mental disability, including hearing, mobility, and visual impairments, chronic alcoholism, chronic mental illness, AIDS, AIDS Related Complex and mental retardation that substantially limits one or more major life activities and you have a record of such a disability or is regarded as having such a disability. The landlord may not refuse to let you make reasonable modifications to the dwelling, at your expense, if needed, for the disabled person. (The landlord may permit changes only if you agree to restore the property to its original condition upon moving.) The landlord also may not refuse to make reasonable accommodations in rules, policies, practices or services, if needed, for the disabled person to use the housing.

NOTE: Housing does not need to be made available to any person who is a direct threat to the health or safety of others or who currently uses illegal drugs.

For more information on fair housing rights or if you feel you have been a victim of discrimination with regard to fair housing, contact the Department of Housing and Urban Development (HUD).

Renters – Your Rights & Responsibilities

With so many people who rent or lease homes or apartments, I felt it necessary to devote a chapter to your rights and responsibilities as a renter. In a perfect world renters and landlords would get along well together and respectfully but the horror stories that I have heard when I worked as a counselor emphasized the need to inform and educate on your rights and responsibilities.

Renter's rights vary by state so you are encouraged to look for specifics pertaining to the state in which you live. However, there are basic rights that are likely to be included in all state tenant-landlord laws. The Fair Housing Act makes it illegal to deny housing to anyone on the grounds of race, color, sex, disability, family status or national origin. The only exception would be units that are developed primarily for seniors, but it is advisable to still check with your state for other exceptions.

Your basic rights are:

1. The right to have a rental unit that is habitable and in compliance with housing and health codes. You should check to be sure the apartment or house is

structurally sound, sanitary, weather-proofed, safe, and is equipped with adequate water, electricity and heating.

2. The right to receive a notice (usually 24 hours) prior to a landlord or maintenance person entering your premises and is limited to making repairs or in case of an emergency.

3. The right to break your lease if the landlord has violated important terms related to health, safety, or necessary repairs.

4. The right to receive an itemized list of deductions from the landlord if the security deposit is not returned to you or has been reduced. The security deposit is not ceductible for "normal wear and tear".

5. The right to receive your refundable portion of the security deposit within 14 to 30 days after vacating the premises, even if you were evicted from the property.

As a tenant, it is also important that you understand what is required of the landlord to be aware if infractions have incurred or your rights have been violated. Again, the laws vary by state so be sure to check with your State Housing Unit on tenant-landlord laws for a complete list. A landlord:

1. Can't stipulate in the lease that the tenant is

responsible for the landlord's attorney fees in case of a court dispute.

2. Can't change the locks nor turn off or cause to be turned off any utilities without prior notice.

3. Can't evict you without a court order notice of eviction.

4. Can't initiate an eviction based on retaliation for actions a tenant takes related to a perceived landlord violation.

5. Can't legally seize a tenant's property for nonpayment of rent or any other reason, except in the case of abandonment as defined by law.

6. Can't make life so miserable for a tenant that you are forced to move out. This may be considered as "constructive eviction", which is grounds for legal action.

7. Must make necessary repairs and perform maintenance tasks in a timely manner or include a provision in the lease that the tenant can order repairs and deduct the cost from the rent.

8. Are limited to the amount of security deposit they can charge for a unit. Check with your state laws for any limitations that may apply.

As you can see, there are rights and responsibilities on both sides when renting. Take the necessary actions before moving in to avoid some of the possible violations discussed. Before moving in, conduct a tour with the landlord of the property that you are considering renting. Take photos of each room and particularly any damage that is noticeable. Bring any concerns to the landlord's attention and request a remediation plan (if they will address the issue, when, etc.). If the unit meets your approval, request a copy of the lease and read it carefully or have an attorney look at it for you. After moving in, keep in mind that you have rights and the responsibility of abiding by the terms of the lease and maintaining the property in habitable condition.

After moving, if your landlord withholds the security deposit, ask for an itemized list of the charges and the reason for the charges. If there is a difference in the list provided by the landlord with your list and pictures taken before moving in, let the landlord know immediately, in writing. Keep copies of all correspondence to and from the landlord, including telephone and in-person conversations. These may be necessary if you are unable to resolve the issue with the landlord yourself.

In the event that legal action becomes necessary or legal action is filed against you by the landlord, seek professional legal help immediately. Check online at your state's Bar Association for a list of referrals to attorneys that handle landlord-tenant disputes. Many offer a free consultation and may have options available for representation at a reduced rate or for no charge, depending on your financial situation. Only choose to pursue legal action as a last resort because it can become expensive alternative.

What's On Your Credit Report?

A consumer credit report is an factual record of your credit activities and can include your personal information (name, address, date of birth, telephone number(s), social security number, city, state, and employer/past employers, as well as your pay history with lenders and creditors (banks, auto loans, mortgage/rent, finance companies, and retail stores). Many of the information found on the credit report comes from lenders who you have had or still have accounts with. When you pay your bills on time or if you fail to pay your bills, lenders report your credit information (good and bad) to credit report agencies.

There are three major credit reporting agencies, Equifax Bureau, TransUnion Bureau, and Experian Bureau. There are two types of credit reports that you can request; a single credit report or a 3-agency credit report. It is advisable to obtain a 3-agency credit report because not all lenders report to all three credit bureaus so there may be information on one that does not show up on another. Each year, you are allowed to request a credit report, for free, from each of the three major credit bureaus. This is advisable since there may be information shown on your credit report that may be inaccurate. You can receive a copy from each bureau at http://www.AnnualCreditReport.com .

The information found on the credit reports, in addition to your personal information and payment history, includes every credit card opened in your name; details of every loan opened in your name; a complete breakdown of your payment history; an account of all the companies that have looked at your credit report (inquiries), and public records such as liens, judgments, and bankruptcy. The importance of reviewing these reports could be significant if someone opened an account in your name and you were unaware of it. While working as a counselor, I was continually amazed at the number of credit reports that were inaccurate and needed to be disputed.

Another important reason for knowing what is on your credit report is that many employers have begun checking credit reports to determine if you are financially responsible. Lenders and landlords check credit reports to see how your payment history with other creditors has been. Unknown to you, thieves may have gotten access to your personal information and made purchases or loans in your name that can affect your credit score significantly. There are credit monitoring services offering 24-hour monitoring to alert you of unauthorized entries to help prevent identity theft or you can check your report diligently to know what is there and if you need to act on inaccurate information.

There are remedies for you if you do find inaccurate information or you wish to dispute an entry that is on your credit report. Each credit reporting bureau has a dispute process that is accessible online where they will investigate the alleged inaccuracy, remove it from your credit report within 30 days, and if found to be inaccurate, the credit reporting bureau may provide a revised credit reports to the last agency or lender that requested a report on your behalf.

Another point that should be mentioned in regards to credit reports is that you should check with each credit reporting bureau on the process to include a consumer statement on your report. Usually there is a limit to how much space is allotted for a consumer statement but it can be very helpful for lenders who may see a series of late payments or even a charge-off and then the consumer statement detailing "during a specific period of time you were laid off from work" or "unable to make monthly payments due to medical illness and hospitalization during a specific period". There is no guarantee that the consumer statement will help your chance of obtaining a loan, but it will give you an opportunity to voice an explanation for delinquencies.

Once your credit report is accurately reflective of your financial payment history, you can then begin to address those entries that may show delinquent to get them back in good standing in order to positively affect your credit score.

Negative entries remain on your credit report until they expire, unless they are found to be inaccurate. Bankruptcies remain on a credit report for 10 years following the discharge of the bankruptcy. Other items remain on the credit report for 7 years from the date of the last activity. (NOTE: The 7 year period starts all over again whenever you generate activity on delinquent account, including making a payment.) If, however, the entry is about to drop off of your credit report and no payments have been made on it during the 7-year period, it cannot be regenerated as new.

Some creditors will attempt to make an old debt new again by reselling the account to an outside collection agency. The Federal Trade Commission (FTC) frowns on this practice and encourages consumers to report the agency to the FTC and notify the creditor (collections) that you are doing so. Many collection agencies take advantage of the fact that many consumers do not know there are laws that protect them or understand their rights as consumers.

The Home Buying Process

Everyone dreams of becoming a homeowner one day. This section will help you to be more educated and equipped about the process and what to expect throughout the process. As we discussed earlier your savings are very important for this process. Every state and every lender has different requirements so be sure to check for your specific state, but some upfront money will be necessary to begin the process of purchasing a home. Most lenders require between a 3.5% to 20% down payment based on the purchase price of what you are interested in buying.

There are some programs that assist first-time homebuyers with closing costs and other fees so be sure to check to see if you qualify. Some lenders also require that you have money set aside that has not been accessed for several months, but the amounts vary. Other funds may be needed for an appraisal ($300 - $500) and closing costs (usually 3% to 5% of purchase price). Your realtor will be able to provide you with an estimation of the closing costs, appraisal fees and any other money you will need. Don't forget to set money aside for moving expenses as well.

After determining that you have adequate funds available to begin the process of homeownership, review your current budget to see how the added expenses will affect your budget and if your income is sufficient to handle purchasing a home. Remember we discussed in an earlier chapter, your housing costs should not exceed 28% of your monthly take-home income. It is a good rule, during this budget review process, to check your credit score for any inaccurate information and to see if your score is high enough for approval. Check with different lenders in your area, letting them know you are considering homeownership and ask about their requirements. You would be surprised at how open they are to sharing this information and some even offer incentives to try to win you as a customer. It is always smart to shop 3-4 different lenders and compare interest rates and approval requirements.

The pre-approval process is the next step in becoming ready to purchase a home. Sellers want to know that you are serious and having a pre-approval letter from a lender gives the assurance that you are indeed "looking to purchase" rather than "just browsing". Most mortgage companies have pre-approval applications online such as Bank of America and Wells Fargo. Lenders will review your financial stability and provide you with a pre-approval letter of the amount of house that you can afford. Remember that the pre-approval does not guarantee that you will obtain a loan but rather lets the lender and the seller know what you can afford. This saves a great deal of time from looking at homes that are out of your price range or over-extending yourself. Congratulate yourself on getting pre-approved. You're not locked into anything at this point; it just lets you know your hard work at becoming financially stable has paid off.

The fun part of the process begins after receiving your pre-approval letter – searching for your new home. A word of caution: Just because you may be approved for a $250,000 house does not mean you have to purchase a $250,000 house. Connect with a local realtor that can show you different properties within your budget, but don't settle on the first, or second, or third home you see. You can also search online for neighborhoods in your area to consider and make a note of them. One website to check is http://www.realestate.yahoo.com/neighborhoods.

My husband and I retained a really good realtor when purchasing our home but still put in the legwork to get out there on our own and search for areas where we wanted to live. Amazingly, my realtor provided great properties to see but we ended up purchasing a home that we found on our own. We contacted our realtor, gave him the address, and he did the rest. This is a major purchase in your life, don't settle for just anything. Take the time and find the home that you will be truly happy with.

After locating the home that you want to purchase, your

realtor will provide you with a "comp" list, which is short for comparable sales. This list will show homes in the area that you are interested in and the sales prices for those sold recently. With the help of your realtor, you can then make an intelligent offer for the home. Don't feel that you are required to offer the asking price. You are in control and by knowing, you're able to negotiate with the seller. Be sure to check to see how long the property has been on the market. This may be able to help you gauge how motivated the seller is to sell the property, giving you a little leverage. Talk with your realtor about including a phrase that the offer is contingent on the outcome of the appraisal and approval of financing. This gives you an out, if needed, without penalty.

Also, don't hesitate to ask for concessions. The worst they can respond with is a "no", but most often the seller may consider your offer fair and accept it. Some things that you may want to consider in your offer is asking the seller to pay all of the closing costs, asking the seller to pay for the appraisal, or asking for money to be put in escrow for repairs. Your realtor will be better able to give ideas of things to ask for in your offer. Remember: Ask not, get not! The seller will visit with their realtor and respond with an acceptance or a counter-offer. They may be willing to pay only half of the closing cost instead of all of it. Either way, you're communicating and they know you're serious.

Once the offer has been accepted and signed by you and the seller, it is important (Very Important) that you have an appraisal conducted of the home you are planning on purchasing. Generally you have 7-10 days to revoke the offer, without penalty, and this is the time to have the appraisal done. An appraiser will conduct a thorough assessment of the home from top to bottom, inside and out and provide you with a report of the stability of the house. Many of the things that an appraiser will identify are things that may not be seen during the tour of the home such as faulty electric wiring (sockets that do not work), foundation problems (cracks in ceilings and walls), weatherproofing around windows, poor insulation, termite infestation, and many other things that you may not discover until after you have moved in. The appraisal will also let you know if the home is worth the price being asked. At that point you can decide if you still want to purchase the property, revise your offer, or walk away. (The law requires a seller to disclose everything that may be wrong with the house up front, but that does not always happen so protect yourself with an appraisal.)

When you decide that you are, indeed, interested in going forward with the purchase of the home, your realtor will help you with getting the paperwork finalized and set up a closing date. You will be required to bring a certified check to the closing to cover any costs that will be paid by the buyer, if any. A broker will be present to go over all of the paperwork to be sure you are fully aware and in agreement with the terms of purchase. Signatures will be obtained from the seller and you, the buyer, and the keys will be handed over. The title for the property will be transferred from the seller to you at this time. At this point, you will have become a homeowner.

Becoming a Homeowner – Rights & Responsibilities

As a new homeowner, you have made an investment that is expected to increase in value and you have rights and responsibilities as a new owner. One major responsibility is to protect and maintain your property. This section will provide you with an overview of many of your responsibilities and rights.

Protecting your property is essential for you and your family. Become familiar with the location of the police and fire departments closest to your neighborhood. Write down phone numbers for these as well as for hospitals in the area in case of an emergency. Fire detectors should be installed, if not already present, near each entrance to a bedroom and it is recommended to have a fire extinguisher near the kitchen or main living area. As you work through protecting your property, devote time to change locks on outside doors and be sure each window has a working lock. An alarm system is advisable and deters thieves from targeting your home. Consider purchasing a fire-proof safe to hold important documents and expensive jewelry, when not worn.

Making sure that you have adequate insurance is also

important in homeownership. Lenders require that each homeowner has hazard insurance and it is generally included in your mortgage payment. In some cases you are able to pay for homeowners insurance outside of the mortgage so be sure to check for the requirements for your property. Check to see if your homeowners insurance contains an inflation rider, which will increase the premiums to cover the value of the house as it increased. If it does not, request a review of your policy to be sure it is enough to cover the current market value of the home.

Another type of insurance to consider includes mortgage life insurance, which will pay off the mortgage in the event of the borrower's death. Home warranties cover the major built-in appliances in the home and mechanical systems and are often provided by the seller for one year after the sale of the property. It may be feasible to look into extending the home warranty after the one year period to provide safety of mind that those unexpected expenses would be covered, in whole or in part. Some homes are located in designated flood zones and, if so, you may be required to purchase a separate insurance to cover floods as it is not usually covered in homeowner's policies.

As you begin enjoying your new home, be sure to maintain it for each season with proper weather-stripping and other ongoing upkeep. It is a good rule of thumb to conduct the following maintenance tasks in the fall and spring to prepare your home for the winter and summer months:

In the Fall: Check weather stripping and caulking around windows and doors. Check for cracks and holes in house s ding, fill with caulking if necessary. Remove window air conditioners or put weatherproof covers over them. Drain outside faucets. Remove leaves from gutters and drain pipes to prevent clogging. Check the roof for leaks, as well as the sealing around vents, skylights, and chimneys. Get heating system serviced and change furnace filter. Drain the hot water heater and remove sediment from the bottom of the tank. Clean refrigerator coils.

In the Spring: Caulk and repaint any outside cracked or peeling paint. Patch or replace all door and window screens. Replace air conditioner filters. Clean dryer vents, stove hoods, and room fans. Check seals of refrigerator and freezer. Clean refrigerator coils and burner surfaces. Change batteries in smoke detectors. Check for inside leaky faucets. Check attic for proper ventilation. Clean drapes and blinds. Clean fireplace.

If you purchased a home that is managed by a Homeowners Association, different rules, rights, and responsibilities apply. Homeowner's Associations (HOA) operate under covenants, conditions, and restrictions

(CC&R). These CC&Rs inform you of all the rules you must follow including when you can play loud music, where you can park your car, what you can and cannot put in your front yard or porch area, and other areas that affect your home. As a part of the HOA, you have voting rights and can vote to change any of the rules that are unfair. Also keep in mind, if any of the CC&Rs are illegal, or are being applied in an illegal fashion, you may consider contacting an attorney rather than waiting to vote at an association meeting. Look closely at your CC&Rs and ask questions to fully understand what is being stated and expected.

An HOA almost always requires monthly fees to cover costs associated with repairing and maintaining the community property, like landscaping. You have the right to question where the HOA fees are applied. In most instances, you must pay your HOA fees and can't stop paying them unless you have taken legal action first. Many homeowners have had liens placed on their homes by HOAs because fees have not been paid. If disagreements arise between you and the HOA , even though they have processes for handling disagreements, you still have the right to retain your own attorney.

As you can see the home buying and ownership process is extensive and may differ from state to state. These tips will help you in understanding the process and enjoying your home w th minimal surprises. Good luck!

###

Thank you so much for purchasing *Personal Finance Your Way*. As a small favor I ask that you leave a comment where you purchased it. None of the information contained in this book should be considered legal advice but is provided as informational only. Please consult an attorney for your state laws if you have questions. Customer feedback is always a very helpful tool for others who may be considering a purchase and your input will be greatly appreciated.

ABOUT THE AUTHOR

S. M. Green was born and lived in Memphis, Tennessee for 25 years. She moved to Dallas, Texas in 2000 to pursue her dreams. After a thirteen-year career in the credit counseling industry, she now devotes part of her days, as a stay-at-home mom, to educating and sharing articles, tips, and e-books on personal money management and living within a budget. She has contributed articles on personal finance and money management to a number of e-zine sites such as EzineArticles.com and WordPress.com. Her relationship with Amazon.com and other online associations provides the perfect forum for reaching a wide range of like-minded consumers. S. M. Green currently lives in Dallas, Texas with her husband and five sons.

Read S. M. Green's Smashwords Interview at https://www.smashwords.com/interview/smgreen.

OTHER BOOKS BY THIS AUTHOR

Please visit Amazon.com, Barnes and Noble, or your favorite book retailer for upcoming books by S. M. Green:

The Travel Series

The Soul of Memphis, Tennessee

40+ Free & Low-Cost Things to Do In Dallas, Texas

Atlanta – A Peach of a Place to Visit (coming June 2014)

Finances and Self Help

Personal Finance Your Way

Other Books:

Played

The Calling (To be released in June 2014)

To contact the author or leave reviews and/or feedback:

http://www.smgreen2271@gmail.com

http://www.facebook.com/sandra.green

http://www.twitter.com/smgreen6

www.ingramcontent.com/pod-product-compliance
Lightning Source LLC
Chambersburg PA
CBHW071812170526
45167CB00003B/1287